PARIS

ART DECO

Cover:
"Folies Shepherdess",
bas-relief depicting
Russian dancer
Lila Nikolska,
Teatre des Folies
Bergère, 1928,
32 Rue Richer,
Paris IXe, France.
Architect:
Jean Plumeret.
Artist:
Maurice Picaud (Pico),
1900—1977.

Right:
commemorative
medallion, 1920s.
Sculptor:
Pierre Turin,
1891—1968.

Opposite:
Bookends, 1930.
Sculptor:
Max Le Verrier,
1891—1973.

Title page:
Max Le Verrier
bookends, plus
twelve volumes of
"Encyclopédie des
arts décoratifs
et industriels
modernes aux
XXième siècle", 1925.

First published in 2023 by Palazzo Editions Ltd
15 Church Road
London, SW13 9HE
www.palazzoeditions.com

Text © 2023 Arnold Schwartzman
Photography, design and layout copyright © 2023 Arnold Schwartzman

Paperback ISBN 9781786751324

Bound and printed in China
10 9 8 7 6 5 4 3 2 1

MIX
Paper | Supporting
responsible forestry
FSC® C008047
FSC
www.fsc.org

CONTENTS

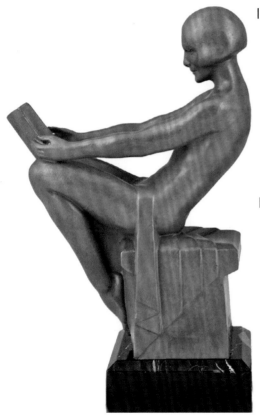

PARIS
ART DECO

ARNOLD

PARIS
ART DECO

SCHWARTZMAN

PALAZZO

La plume de ma tante

Among my most cherished mementos is a 1920s wedding photograph of members of my great aunt's Paris family, the Tenenbaums.

The large group includes my mother who was visiting from her home in London. The smiling "English Rose" is flanked by two admiring cousins.

As a survivor of the destruction of our home during the London Blitz, I was surprised to learn that unlike London where my playground was a bombsite, the French capital had thankfully not suffered the same fate as war-torn London.

This could not be said for the fortunes of a number of French citizens featured in the Jewish wedding photograph.

As a young boy my mother beguiled me with her experience of visiting Paris, which included her description of the remains of the 1925 *Exposition Internationale des Arts Décoratifs et Industriels Modernes*, the exhibition that highlighted the style of the new era.

My mother's memories of Paris enchanted me to the extent that I would have recurring dreams of boarding the boat train and tumbling down a chute with the luggage but never quite arriving at my destination.

My longing to visit the City of Light finally became a reality one day in 1947 when at age eleven, I had the good fortune to be invited to spend my summer holiday with my Great Aunt and Uncle in Paris. My father drove me down to Dover where I boarded the cross-channel ferry to Calais.

I disembarked at the Normandy coast where only three years previously the D-Day invasion had taken place. Along with the other passengers I had to step across several railway tracks to board the SNCF steam train on to Paris's Gare du Nord railway station.

During the several hours train journey, I passed my time by reading over and over the railway compartment's door sign warning passengers not to lean out of the window, which was printed in three different languages. I can still recite from memory the Italian tongue twister, *"E pericoloso sporgersi"*!

On finally reaching the Paris terminus, I was warmly greeted by my Great Aunt who transported me to her family home in the city's suburb of Savigny-sur-Orge.

Shortly after acclimating to my surroundings I was given the responsibility to visit the local *boulangerie* to purchase loaves of *baguettes* and *fromage* for our *petit déjeuner*.

My family wedding group, Paris 1920s.

Circled:
top center,
My mother
Rose, right,
my great aunt
Rosa Tenenbaum,
bottom left,
my cousin
Alexandre, who
some two decades
later, now a
schoolteacher,
became my tour
guide during my
first visit to Paris.

As an aspiring designer I appreciated the graphic labels that adorned the Camembert cheese boxes; the same could not be said for the contents' odor! I was further given instructions not to patronize the shops owned by former Nazi collaborators.

My aunt's younger son, Alexandre, a seasoned schoolteacher, became my guide to the city. Our first stop was the iconic Eiffel Tower, where from *le premier étage* we observed the panoramic vista of Paris, my guide pointing out that across the River Seine was the site of the former Palais du Trocadero, since demolished to make way for the "Moderne" style Palais de Chaillot, built for the 1937 Exposition Internationale.

This exhibition was preceded by the 1925 *Exposition Internationale des Arts Décoratifs et Industriels Modernes*, which ushered in the style known today as "Art Deco". This style blossomed from Manhattan to Morecambe and beyond, bringing about yet another industrial revolution.

In the wake of the 1922 discovery of Tutankhamen's tomb, Egyptomania spawned a plethora of Egyptian-style *object de'art* and architecture.

The Art Deco movement, having drawn inspiration from Aztec and Japanese cultures,

influenced the design of fabrics, furniture, radios, glassware, jewelry, and graphics, and last but not least, architecture.

Our tour included visits to several *grande magazins* including *Au Printemps* and *Aux Galleries Lafayette*, allowing me to exchange my five pound allowance into *francs*.

On our visit to the Palais de Chaillot, I blushed at the sight of the nude golden statuettes adorning the Palais's plaza. The very thought of the possibility of attending a *Follies Bergere* performance of semi-naked ladies would bring on a further bloom to my cheeks. Not to mention the *bouquinistes* (peasants of Paris), their cabinets lining the banks of the Seine full of collections of *risqué* ephemera and postcards.

"Don't know much about the French I took…"

I frequently purchased postcards of the numerous sites that I had visited to mail home to my parents. My trips to the local *Tabac* to purchase *poste cartels* (*sic*) would often bring a smile to the shopkeeper's face. So much for *"French without tears"*, as it would appear that I had put the *carte* before the *cheval*!

Page from the author's British passport with Bureau de change stamps from Aux Galleries Lafayette and Au Printemps, 1947.

9

It was not to be for another twenty years that I had the opportunity to revisit the metropolis.

This time, armed with my Voigtlander Bellows camera, I viewed Paris in a different light. At art school I had learnt a rudimentary history of architecture from Bannister Fletcher's "History of Architecture". From this basic tutorial I could differentiate between the Art Nouveau movement from that of Art Deco.

My foremost interest has been to document the beautiful florid architectural details that adorn these buildings, the doors, balconies, bas-reliefs and graphics. The pride taken by these architects in their structures is endorsed by the inclusion of their names

carved into the façades of their creations.

The iconographic imagery of the *Art Nouveau* era depicted prides of peacocks,

AUX GALERIES

LE PAVILLON DES
CRÉÉ E
PAR "LA
L'EXPOSI
DÉCORA
· PA

swarms of dragonflies and a bevy of swans, these were superseded by herds of leaping fawns, swoops of swallows and a pack of

Afghan hounds, augmented by a splash of fountains and a fleet of Zeppelins.

The last time I saw Paris...

Missing were the *gendarmes' champêtre kepi*, the circular hats as worn by "Inspector Clouseau" in the *Pink Panther* films. Also gone was the ability to hop on and off the open back platforms of the vintage Renault green buses. In my rides in a Citroen taxi I was intrigued to learn that the drivers were often Russian princes in exile, expressing their newfound freedom by producing a symphony with their klaxon horns, *à la* a Gershwin tune.

An American in Paris

Opposite:
View of Sacre Coéur Basilica through the face of the giant clock of Gare d'Orsay, 1900, the former railway station.
1 Rue de la Légion d'Honneur,
Paris, France.
Architects:
Victor Laloux,
1850—1937,
Lucien Magne,
1849—1016,
Émile Bénard,
1844—1929.

Above:
A page from the author's US passport, 2022.

It has been seventy plus years since my first visit to Paris when I was comforted with the knowledge that my British passport stated "We, Ernest Bevin, a Member of his Britannic Majesty's most Honourable Privy Council, a Member of Parliament, etc, etc.

His Majesty's Principal Secretary of State for Foreign Affairs, request and require in the name of His Majesty all those whom it may concern to allow the bearer to pass without let or hindrance and to afford him every assistance and protection of which he may stand in need".

This time sporting my American passport, my mission was to supplement my earlier photographs of the Capital for this book.

My train Journey from London "sans let or hindrance" or "mal de mer" travelled speedily under the English Channel by Eurostar, arriving once more at Paris's Gare du Nord railway station.

At the bureau de change I exchanged my U.S. dollars for Euros then I went on to enjoy once more the architectural treasures and gastronomic delights of the City of Light.

Right:
"Folies Shepherdess",
bas-relief depicting
Russian dancer
Lila Nikolska,
Teatre des Folies
Bergère, 1928,
32 Rue Richer,
Paris IXe, France.
Architect:
Jean Plumeret.
Artist:
Maurice Picaud (Pico),
1900—1977.

Far right:
Poster, "Le passé dans
le retró", ca. 1926.
Artist:
Maurice Picaud (Pico).

Today one can find the once flaking bas-reliefs of the Follies
Bergére's façade shimmering in gold.

Allow me to *ouvre la porte* to virtually guide you through
some of the oft-unnoticed "Decotecture"
treasures of Paris. **Bon appetit!**

14

"Folies Shepherdess",
bas-relief, restored
to its original color,
depicting Russian
dancer
Lila Nikolska,
Teatre des Folies
Bergère, 1928,
32 Rue Richer,
Paris, France.
Artist:
Maurice Picaud (Pico).

Poster, 1937,
Exposition Internationale.
Artists:
Eugene Baudouin,
1898—1983,
Marcel Lods,
1891—1978.

SCULPTURE

The Eiffel Tower
viewed from the
promenade of the
Palais de Chaillot,
1937.
Place du Trocadéro,
Paris, France.
Architects:
Jacques Carlu,
Louis-Hippolyte
Boileau,
Léon Azéma,
1888—1978.

Gilded statues,
Le Printemps, 1937.
Sculptor:
Paul Niclauesse,
1879—1958.
Far right:
Flore, 1937.
Sculptor:
Marcel Gimond,
1894—1961.
Palais de Chaillot,
Place du Trocadéro,
Paris, France.

18

Gilded statues,
Far left:
La Jeunesse, 1937.
Sculptor:
Alexandre
Descatoire,
1874—1949.
Left:
Les fruits, 1937.
Sculptor:
Louis Brasseur,
1879—1960.
Palais de Chaillot,
Place du Trocadéro,
Paris, France.

Gilded statues,
Right:
Le Matin, 1937.
Sculptor:
de Pryas.
Far right:
La Campagne, 1937.
Sculptor:
Paul Cornet,
1892—1977.
Palais de Chaillot,
Place du Trocadéro,
Paris, France.

Sculpture,
La Jeunesse,
Fontaine de Varsovie,
Place du Trocadéro,
Palais de Chaillot,
Paris, France.
Sculptor:
Pierre-Marie Poisson.
1876—1953.

Taureau et Daim,
Bronze bull's head
and deer sculpture,
1937,
Fontaine de Varsovie,
Place du Trocadéro,
Palais de Chaillot,
Paris, France.
Sculptor:
Paul Jouve,
1878—1973.

Horse and dog
sculptures,
Jardins du Trocadéro,
Palais Chaillot,
Paris, France.
Sculptor:
Georges Guyot,
1885—1973.

Above:
Mascaron,
(ornamental face), 1937,
and right:
Pomone,
Place du Trocadéro,
Palais de Chaillot,
Paris, France.
Sculptor:
Robert Wiérick,
1882—1944.

Apollo with harp,
bas relief,
Teatre de Chaillot,
Place du Trocadéro,
Palais de Chaillot,
Paris, France.
One of a number of
Greek and Roman
mythological
sculptures.

Bronze statue,
Hercule et le
Taureau,
(Hercules and
the Bull), 1937.
Place du Trocadéro,
Palais de Chaillot,
Paris, France.
Sculptor:
Albert Pommier,
1880—1943.

Bronze with harp,
Apollon Musagète,
1937.
Palais de Chaillot,
Place du Trocadéro,
Paris, France.
Sculptor:
Albert Pommier.

Detail, bas relief,
"Indochine", 1937,
terrace,
Palais de Chaillot,
Place du Trocadéro,
Paris, France.
Sculptor:
Anna Quinquaud,
1890—1984.

Detail, bas relief,
Art Français
(French Art), 1937,
terrace,
Palais de Chaillot,
Place du Trocadéro,
Paris, France.
Sculptor:
Charles Hairon
1880–1962.

Above:
French postage stamp,
Antoine Bourdelle
"La Danse",
Stamp designer:
Jacques Combet,
1920—1993.

Right:
"La danse",
Isadora Duncan
et Nijinsky, 1913,
bas relief,
façade of
Théâtre des
Champs Elysées,
Paris, France.
Sculptor:
Antoine Bourdelle
1861—1929.

"La musique", 1913,
bas relief,
façade of Théâtre
des Champs Elysées,
Paris, France.
Sculptor:
Antoine Bourdelle.

"La comédie" 1913,
bas relief,
façade of Théâtre des
Champs Elysées,
Paris, France.
Sculptor:
Antoine Bourdelle
1861—1929.

"La tragédie", 1913,
bas relief,
façade of Théâtre
des Champs Elysées,
Paris, France.
Sculptor:
Antoine Bourdelle
1861—1929.

37

Right:
Poster,
Exposition Coloniale
Internationale, 1931.
Artist:
Jean Victor Desmeures,
1895—1978.

Opposite:
Granite sculpture of
two lionesses, 1931.
Sculptor:
Henri Navarre,
1885—1970.

Previous spread:
Façade,
Palais de la
Porte Dorée,
293 Avenue Daumesnil,
Paris, France.
Architects:
Albert Laprade,
1883—1978,
Léon Jaussely,
1875—1932.
Sculptor:
Alfred Janniot,
1889—1969.

Built in 1931 for the
Colonial Exposition.
It now houses the
Musée de l'Histoire
de l'Immigration, as
well as a tropical
aquarium in its cellar.

This page and
opposite:
Façade details.

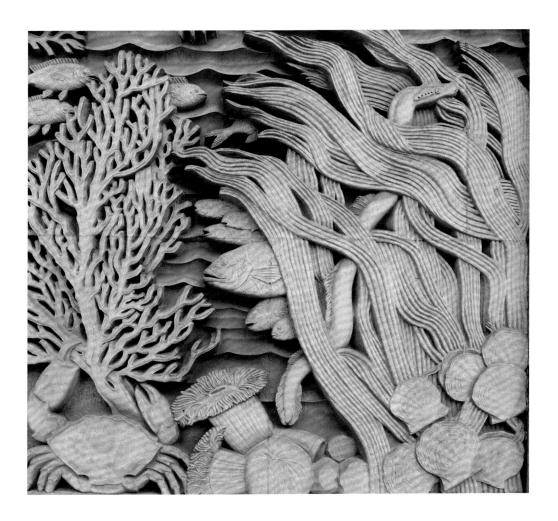

Above:
Postage stamp,
Exposition Coloniale
Internationale de Paris,
1931.

Right:
Façade,
Palais de la
Porte Dorée,
293 Avenue Daumesnil,
Paris, France.
Architects:
Albert Laprade,
1883–1978,
Léon Jaussely,
1875–1932,
Sculptor:
Alfred Janniot,
1889–1969.

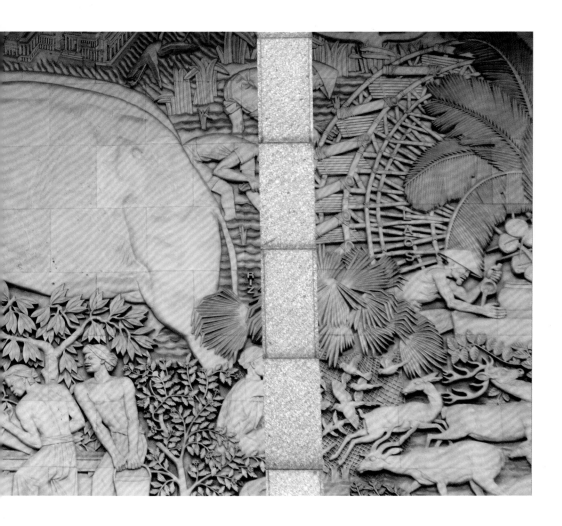

Façade detail,
bas relief, "Marseilles",
Palais de la
Porte Dorée,
293 Avenue Daumesnil,
Paris, France.
Architects:
Albert Laprade,
1883—1978,
Léon Jaussely,
1875—1932,
Sculptor:
Alfred Janniot,
1889—1969.

Façade detail,
bas relief, "Bordeaux",
Palais de la
Porte Dorée,
293 Avenue Daumesnil,
Paris, France.
Architects:
Albert Laprade,
1883—1978,
Léon Jaussely,
1875—1932,
Sculptor:
Alfred Janniot,
1889—1969.

Façade detail.
Palais de la
Porte Dorée,
293 Avenue Daumesnil,
Paris, France.
Architects:
Albert Laprade,
1883—1978,
Léon Jaussely,
1875—1932,
Sculptor:
Alfred Janniot,
1889—1969.

Medallion,
Exposition Coloniale
Internationale,
Paris, 1931.
Sculptor:
Lucien Bazor,
1889—1974.

Monument à la
Mission Marchand.
Bas relief of the
expeditionary force
of Jean Baptiste-
Marchand, 1934.
1b Avenue Daumesnil,
Paris, France.
Sculptors:
Roger-Henri Expert,
1882—1955,
Léon Georges Baudry,
1898—1978.

FACHODA
10 JUILLET 1898

BAHR EL GHAZAL

TAMBOURA

DJIBOUTI

MAI 1899

AU
COMMANDANT
MARCHAND
CHEF
DE LA MISSION CONGO NIL

AUX MEMBRES DE L'EXPEDITION :
CAPITAINE BARATIER
LIEUTENANT LARGEAU
LIEUTENANT MOUGE

1930s "Flappers",
low reliefs,
private residence.
Paris, France.

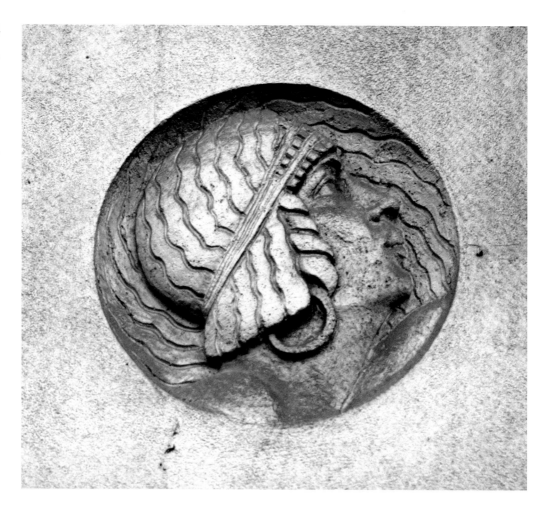

53

Keystone bas relief,
private residence,
Paris, France.
Architect:
Paul-Jacques-Aimé
Baudry.

Keystone bas relief,
private residence,
Paris, France.

Façade,
Le Samaritaine
department store,
1926—1928,
19 Rue de la Monnaie,
Paris, France,
Architects:
Henri Sauvage,
1873—1932,
Frantz Jourdain,
1847—1935.

FAÇADES

Sculptural reliefs,
façade,
residential building,
1913, 65–67
Blvd Raspail,
Paris, France.
Architect:
Léon Tissier.
Sculptor:
Louis Henri Bouchard
1875–1960.

Louxor Cinema, 1920,
170 Blvd de Magenta,
Paris, France.
Architect:
Henri Zipcy.
1873–1950.

Inspired by the 1917
silent film "Cleopatra".

Ornano 43 Theatre,
1933,
43 Blvd Ornano,
Paris, France.
Architect:
Marcel Oudin.

Le Raspail, 1964,
216 Blvd Raspail,
Paris, France.
Architect:
Bruno Elkouken,
1893–1968.

Palais du Hanovre,
now BNP PARIBAS,
1932,
25–34 Rue Louis
Legrande.
Paris, France.
Architects:
Victor Laloux,
Charles-Henri-Camille
Lemaresquier,
1870—1972.

Central tower,
private residence.

65

Interior,
Brasserie Vaudeville,
1918,
29 Rue Vivienne,
Paris, France.
Architects:
Solvet Père et Fils.

INTERIORS

Right and
opposite:
Interior,
Brasserie Vaudeville,
1918,
29 Rue Vivienne,
Paris, France.
Architects:
Solvet Père et Fils.

Minister Reynaud
Room, Palais de la
Porte Dorée, 1931,
293 Avenue
Daumesnil,
Paris, France.
Interior design:
Jacques-Emile
Ruhlmann,
1879—1933.

MURALS

Frescoes:
Muralist
Louis Bouquet,
1885—1952 .

Details of four murals,
Palais de la
Porte Dorée, 1931,
293 Avenue
Daumesnil,
Paris, France.
Frescos:
Pierre Ducos
de la Haille,
1886–1972.

Right:
"Science",
Far right:
"Travail".

Far left:
"Commerce,
Left:
"Liberté".

73

Detail,
Post Office, 1925,
22 Rue de Provence
and Rue Chauchat,
Paris, France.

DECORATION

Decorative detail,
residential building.

This page and overleaf: Decorative detail, residential building.

This page and opposite: Decorative detail, residential building.

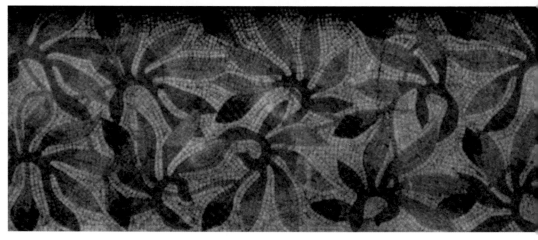

This page and
opposite:
Decorative
metal grilles.

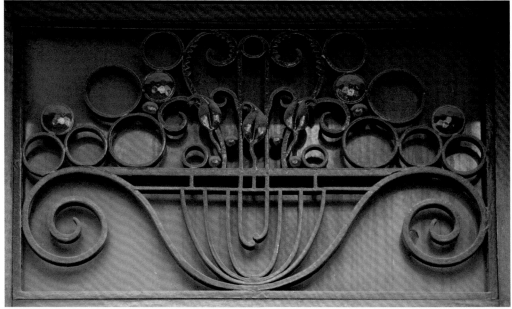

MOSAICS

Mosaic decoration,
Kahn Boulangerie,
24 Rue des Ecouffes,
Paris, France.

Mosaic facade,
residential building.

Detail,
mosaic facade,
residential building.

Mosaic Parisian
street sign.

Mosaic,
horsemeat
butcher shop.
Rue du Roi de Sicile,
Le Marais,
Paris, France.

Mosaics,
former butcher shop,
9 Rue de Duras,
Paris, France.

Detail,
Mosaic floor,
Lecreux Frères
funeral home,
37 Blvd de
Ménilmontant,
Paris, France.

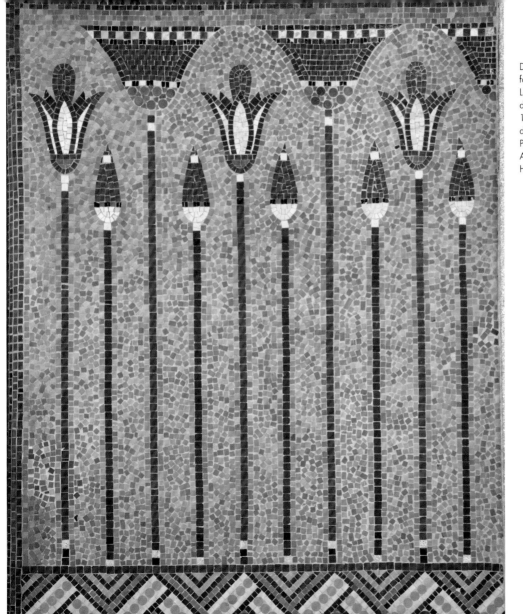

Detail, mosaic,
façade,
Louxor Palais
du Cinema, 1921,
170 Boulevard
de Magenta,
Paris, France.
Architect:
Henri Zipcy.

Street numbers, 1913,
65–67 Blvd Raspail,
Paris, France.
Architect:
Léon Tissier.
Sculptor:
Louis Henri Bouchard.

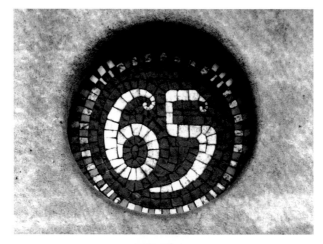

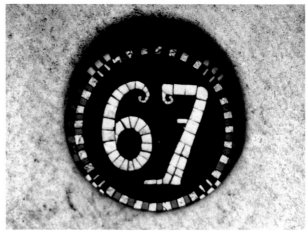

Mosaic street signs.

Detail,
Mosaic frieze,
Le Samaritaine
department store,
1926—1928,
19 Rue de la
Monnaie,
Paris, France,
Architects:
Henri Sauvage,
Frantz Jourdain.

Detail, mosaic,
façade,
Louxor Palais
du Cinema, 1921,
170 Boulevard
de Magenta,
Paris, France.
Architect:
Henri Zipcy.

Paris displays an artistic array of wrought iron balconies.

BALCONIES

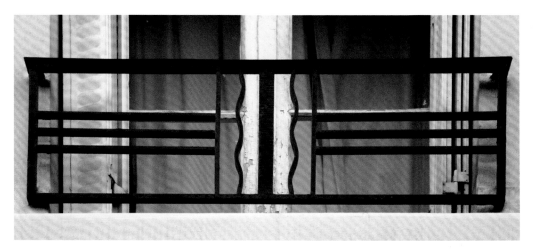

106

117

Etched glass screen,
Brasserie Vaudeville,
1918,
29 Rue Vivienne,
Paris, France.
Architects:
Solvet Père et Fils.

GLASS

Detail,
decorated frosted
glass door,
main entrance,
Folies Bergère,
1928.
32 Rue Richer,
Paris, France.

Painted frosted glass window, 1930s. Passage Jouffroy, 10 Blvd Montmartre, Paris, France.

Right:
Beurre-Laiterie-Oeufs,
Creamery, 1930s.
25 Rue Danielle
Casanova,
Paris, France.
Opposite:
Livarot, Camembert
cheese box label,
1928.

SIGNAGE

Overleaf:
Facade,
butcher's shop.
Paris, France.

FERME DU BLANC-GÂTEL
LIVAROT
AU BON
PETIT BOISSEY
Rouen
Prix, Médaille d'Or
PARIS
de Vermeil, Caen
MAURICE GUIBÉ Fabricant à Boissey

Above:
Medallion, telephonist,
1920s.
Sculptor:
André Pierre Schwab,
1883–unknown.

Right:
Ministère des PTT,
telephone exchange,
1928,
11 Rue d'Edimbourg,
Paris, France.
Architect:
Charles Giroud,
1871–1955.

Book store Librairie
EYROLLES, L'École
spéciale des travaux
publics, du bâtiment
et de l'industrie
(ESTP Paris).
59 Blvd Saint Germain,
Paris, France.

Signage,
Le Samaritaine
department store,
1926—1928,
19 Rue de la
Monnaie,
Paris, France,
Architects:
Henri Sauvage,
Frantz Jourdain.

Mosaic decoration,
Florence Kahn
Boulangerie, 1932,
24 Rue des Ecouffes,
Paris, France.

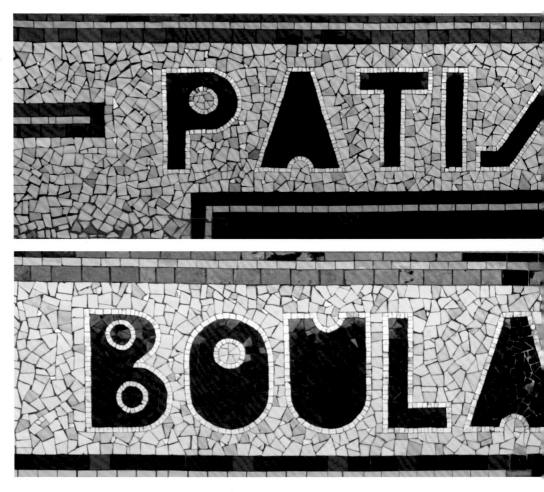

Signage,
Lecreux Frères
funeral home,
37 Blvd de
Ménilmontant,
Paris, France.

Overleaf:
Metal signage,
former pharmacy,
1930s,
91 Saint Germain
Blvd.,
Paris, France.

Painted signs, fruit
and vegetable shop.

Metal and glass
door sign,
service entrance,
private residence..

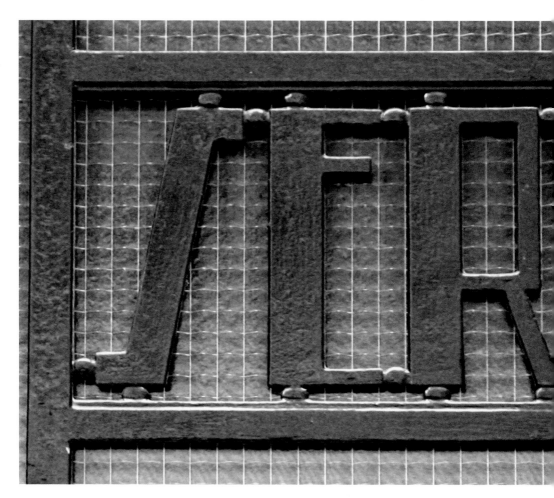

Painted sign, shoe shop.

Painted sign, food store.

140

Wood sign, fruit and
vegetable shop.

Wood sign,
hardware shop.

Painted sign,
paint shop.
6 rue Tombouctou,
Paris, France.

Metal on marble sign,
butcher shop, 1930s,
17 Rue des Rosiers,
Paris, France.

144

Paris displays a vast
creative array of
wrought iron doors.

DOORS

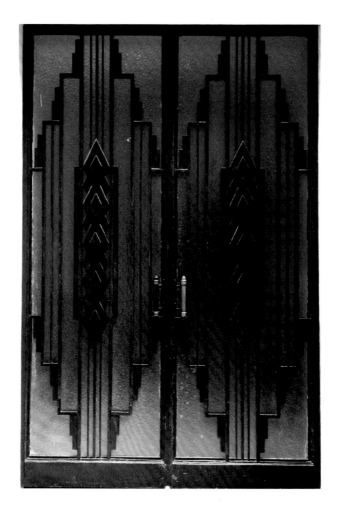

150

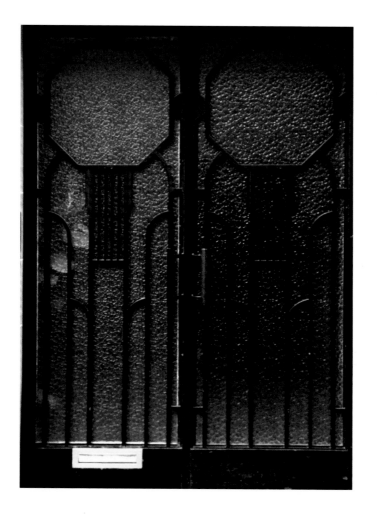

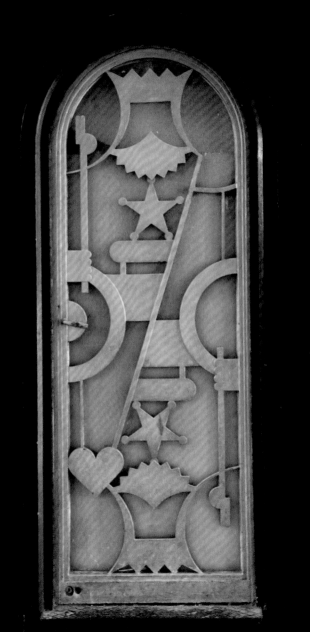

Brass door, 1930s.
Passage Jouffroy,
10 Blvd Montmartre,
Paris, France.

Studio building,
1926—28,
2–4 Rue du
Général Largeau,
Paris, France.
Architect:
Henri Sauvage
1873—1932.
Ceramic tiles:
Gentil et Bourdet.

Right:
Silver medallion,
1920s.
Sculptor:
Pierre Turin.
1891—1968 .

Far right:
Pochoir print (stencil),
Au Revoir,
detail from
Le Bonheur du Jour, ou
Les Graces à la Mode,
1924.
Artist:
George Barbier,
1882—1932.

Acknowledgments

With special thanks to my wife and creative partner
Isolde for her diligent attention to
the production of this book.

With grateful thanks to:
Marie-France Droiun
Roberta Nusim
Harry Peccinotti
Rosine Tenenbaum
Michael Webb

Au revoir...

Passport photograph of the author age 11 on his first visit to Paris, 1947.

London-born Arnold Schwartzman OBE RDI, is a renowned graphic designer, documentary film-maker, author and educator.

His career began as a title designer in broadcast television and as a regular illustrator and design consultant to the *Sunday Times* magazine, London.

He later became an advertising agency art director producing award winning commercials for Coca-Cola. In 1974 he was elected a member of the Alliance Graphique Internationale.

In 1978 he was invited to Hollywood by legendary designer Saul Bass to become his studio's design director. Bass later recommended him to make a documentary on the subject of the Holocaust which resulted in Arnold receiving the Academy Award® as the producer and director of the 1981 feature documentary, *Genocide*.

In 1982 he was appointed the director of design for the Los Angeles 1984 Olympic Games. Schwartzman is the designer of two murals for Cunard's "Queen Elizabeth" cruise ship, and the "UN Peace Bell Memorial", Seoul, Korea. In 2002 he was appointed an Officer of the Order of the British Empire, OBE, and in 2006 was conferred the distinction of Royal Designer, RDI.

The author of a number of books on the subject of 19th and 20th century architecture, *Paris Art Deco* is his third companion book on the Art Deco style.

Arnold lives in Los Angeles and works in collaboration with his wife, Isolde.